life lessons
for leaders

Derric Johnson

wesleyan
publishing
house

Indianapolis, Indiana

Copyright © 2009 by Derric Johnson
Published by Wesleyan Publishing House
Indianapolis, Indiana 46250
Printed in the United States of America
ISBN: 978-0-89827-426-4

To all the men of DREAM BUILDERS #1 in Orlando, Florida, without whose prodding, encouragement, and support this project never would have been completed:

Kennan Burch, founder and president
Randy Alligood, Jim Bauer, Brian Cline, Kris Den Besten,
Tim DeTellis, Bob Faust, Steve French, Steven Grimes,
Tim Grosshans, Jeff Lawrence, Hilgardt Lamprecht,
Mitch Madden, Hank Miller, Eddy Moratin, Bruce Norris,
Mark Starcher, Charles Thomas, and Brent Sapp

And to all the uncommon people
Marching toward an uncommon goal
With an uncommon faith
In an uncommon God,
Who leads them in uncommon paths
Toward an uncommon destiny

contents

Orval Butcher—special, influential, and unique.

To his world . . .

A *man* whose faith in the Savior is more than inspiring; it is contagious.

A *leader* whose dream of what a church could, should, and would be captivates the spirits and hearts of all who know him.

An *example* whose love of life and compassion for ministry have penetrated the souls and saturated the lives of every acquaintance and friend.

But to me personally . . .

I remember his hospitality when my young family lived in his parsonage for three weeks before the miracle of Auntie Vi.

I remember the extra eggs and toast for breakfast when I would just "drop in."

I remember cutting the church lawn, washing his car, and the 5:30 a.m. construction mornings on the Sunday school addition.

I remember the prayers and plans and successes as we did things no one had ever done before.

I remember the youth camps, the songs, and the drives together.

I remember the living nativity scenes—chasing sheep and corralling donkeys.

I remember the Palm Sundays with the children processing down the center aisle, carrying the branches of praise we had cut.

I remember the Easter services on the lower parking lot and then at Mt. Miguel stadium.

I remember the counseling and advice and the forced apologies to young people who had gotten out of line, but somehow, I had to take the blame.

I remember the discipline of getting to the church office at 5:30 in the morning so I could use Janet Beardsley's typewriter before she needed it at 8:00.

I remember mixing mimeograph ink to just the right shade for our Gestetner, so the missionary fliers would be perfect.

I remember the recording sessions, the radio programs, and the Kids' Krusades—complete with parades and ice cream.

I remember the patience and gentleness expressed to a young, aspiring minister; you took a bush and carefully shaped him into a tree.

Orval Butcher, you are the most respected person in my memory.

As we go through life, we meet a lot of different types of people. Some are *question marks*; others provide *commas* to break the flow of energy; and there are the *periods*, who want to stop everything—you remember, the people who think nothing should be done for the first time. There are *quotation marks*, who never think of anything original; and *apostrophes*, who condense and compress everything into contractions (if not contradictions).

But you, in the punctuation of life, you are forever—to me and to the world—an *exclamation point*!

Thanks—in Jesus' name and for His sake.

—DERRIC JOHNSON,
A dedicated disciple

Thanks to . . .

My wonderful partner and patient wife, Debbie, who was the first to listen, suggest, and correct a myriad of "lessons" . . . because we started with over a hundred and fifty items that needed to be culled, sorted, and then ultimately included.

My great friend and wordsmith, Gail Romaine, who sacrificed time and added inspiration to this whole endeavor . . . both for her love of Pastor Orval Butcher and the thrill of helping create this tribute.

To the world, you might be one person . . .
But to one person, you might be the world.

If you can't see it before you see it,
you'll never see it.

In 1953, Pastor Orval Butcher stood on a windblown hill with his friend Eldred Perkins. They looked out on a lovely valley just outside San Diego. This valley soon would be transformed into an entirely new community, with thousands of people ready to move into homes that would eventually be constructed and to start shopping in stores that were yet to be built.

Pastor Butcher was preparing to leave the traveling ministry that had taken him around the world, and he was looking for just the right place to begin the pastoral phase of his life. He had received offers from nine different congregations, as well as from conferences of four denominations, to serve in whatever capacity he would choose.

As he and Eldred prayed that day, he said, "I can see a mighty church, a lighthouse for Jesus, right here on this property. I can see it."

Money was given to buy the property, which was immediately mortgaged to finance the raising of the first building. Volunteers worked evenings and Saturdays with the men digging, sawing, hammering, and painting, while the women prepared meals and varnished chairs.

Before the building was completed, two thousand Christmas cards went out into the community, calls were made, and invitations were extended. The first Sunday the sanctuary was opened, one hundred seventy people turned out. That was the smallest attendance Skyline ever experienced. It was all "up" from there.

It all started with one man who *saw* it—and then knew how to put the pieces together. Only those who see the invisible can do the impossible.

> *Doubt sees the obstacles.*
> *Vision sees the way!*
> *Doubt sees the darkness.*
> *Vision sees the day!*
> *Doubt dreads to take a step.*
> *Vision soars on high!*
> *Doubt questions, "Who believes?"*
> *Vision answers, "I."*

Hard work is anything you do with
no goal in sight.

Visions and goals are two very different things. *Vision* is
like a lighthouse that illuminates. It gives direction. Vision
is a consciously created fantasy of what we would like our
work and ministry to be. It's like a waking dream. A *goal* is a
baby step toward the vision.

A vision comes from the heart; a goal comes from the
head. A positive, meaningful vision of the future supported by
compelling goals provides purpose and direction in the present.

Goals and visions are like stars. You will not succeed in
touching them with your hands. But like a seafaring man on

the waters, you choose them as your guides. By following them you will reach your destiny.

When I arrived on the scene as youth pastor at Skyline Wesleyan Church, the vision for the youth ministry was to create a vibrant group of teens grounded in biblical principles—a group who would be life-changers in their world. The vision included both quality *and* quantity. Looking over the sixteen students who were already in the program, I discovered we had two seniors, one junior, and thirteen sophomores.

The vision was of a large group. Specific goals were necessary to make this happen, so I asked Pastor Butcher for group-building advice. His instruction was simple: "Go for the sophomores."

The reason was that seniors would be moving on in a relatively few months; the future strength of the organization was still growing up. So he insisted that we keep the two seniors happily involved, but without planning any events specifically for them. For example, instead of a graduation banquet for the seniors, we would arrange a more inclusive occasion for the whole group, while paying for the seniors to attend the Youth for Christ year-end extravaganza.

How right Pastor Butcher was! By establishing the goal of strengthening the sophomores, the vision of a larger group came into being. Two years later we had forty-eight seniors (grown-up sophomores), and we kept building from there.

You can smell the compliments; just
don't inhale them.

Our youth ministry at Skyline had just hit the goal of one hundred in attendance for the high school Sunday school class (actually 104). It had taken a couple of years, but now there was the number for all to see, proving that God answers prayer when it is coupled with good old hard work. Pastor Butcher announced the milestone during the evening service and had all the high school students stand amid raucous audience applause.

The next afternoon at 2:15 he called me to his office. "Let's go get a Coke at Oscar's . . . your car." That sounded good to me. I always enjoyed any one-on-one time with him.

At ten minutes till three he remarked, "Let's head up Sweetwater Drive to Mount Miguel High School. We'll sit and watch. There's something I want to show you."

After driving there, I parked the car and waited. When the final school bell rang at three, we watched students race for lockers, bikes, and cars. The commotion at the front of the school reminded me of an anthill that had been topped off by an errant golf swing. There was helter-skelter movement. We stared for six astounding minutes.

Then Pastor Butcher asked me, "How many students are here at Mount Miguel?"

"I'd guess about four thousand."

"Actually, it's 4,126. I called the principal, Mel Grant, to check on it this morning."

"How many did you have yesterday in Sunday school?"

"104."

"And that was really great, Pastor Derric. Now, let's go up the hill and get back to work."

The lesson? He let me bask in a few moments of ecstatic glory, then put things back in precise focus as we viewed what was yet to be done.

Success is to be measured by what you've done with your potential.

It's more important to be significant
than it is to be relevant.

I first heard Pastor Butcher preach when I was a student at Azusa Pacific University. He was the special speaker and spiritual leader for an "all-school revival." His messages were so engaging and challenging that I can remember most of them to this very day. Who could escape his heart-opening version of the Good Samaritan, presented with three characters: the *conceded* Christian, the *conceited* Christian, and the *concerned* Christian? Or his hilarious, yet very pointed, study of the devil's bugaboos?

Note-taking has always been a learning-passion of mine, so when I came to Skyline, I was intrigued by the thought of sitting on the platform every Sunday listening to Pastor Butcher's stirring messages. I was surprised when sermon after sermon passed by, leaving me hardly more than a date, title, and Scripture reference on my 4 x 6 card. I felt I must be missing something.

Since being at Skyline was to be a learning experience, I felt a properly positioned question might be in order, so I risked one: "Pastor Butcher, you seem to speak differently when you're away from your pulpit than you do here. Is there a reason for that?"

He smiled and simply said, "Virtually all the people who attend Skyline are brand-new believers—or at least are trying to be believers—so they will always hear just three things from me:

1. God loves you.
2. Jesus died for you.
3. I care about you.

"I can hire people to come in as prophecy experts, revival specialists, Bible scholars, and family issue authorities, but I can never hire anyone to love my people. That's my job."

Then I heard him say for the first time (remember, this is almost fifty years ago), "People don't care how much you know until they know how much you care."

He didn't just *preach* about that, he *lived* it—every day and with everybody. The most important thing he ever taught me was to really genuinely care. Find a need and touch it.

determination

If you're going to dream,
dream big.

"I'm going to win this community for Christ or die trying. If you feel any differently than that, you might as well pack up tonight and leave in the morning."

Those words were spoken to me at two in the morning during the first week I was at Skyline. My family and I were staying in the Butchers' parsonage until we could find suitable housing, meaning anything with a roof and four walls. We had been talking long into the evening about his vision for this church that God had ordained.

I was young, enthusiastic, and full of energy for the task and dream of ministry. After graduating from Azusa Pacific University, I accepted the opportunity to serve in a small church in the Deep South. The people were wonderful and the building very nice, but comfort seemed to be their primary concern. The message I often heard was "We don't need to take this outreach thing too seriously."

Youth ministry was part of my job description there, and to most people that meant I should just babysit their kids. I wanted to change their world—*now*—but immediacy was not in their church vocabulary. Still, I learned a lot while serving there. As a number-two man, I had great opportunity without great responsibility.

Coming to Skyline, the mood was a 180-degree change. Opportunity abounded and the spiritual need of the community was overwhelming.

Sitting in that parsonage den, I thought Pastor Butcher had fallen asleep. His head was leaning back in a big wing chair. His eyes were closed, and he hadn't moved for ten minutes. The fire was still smoldering in the fireplace, and I was ready to get up and head for bed without disturbing him (not wise to wake a sleeping giant). Suddenly, he sat straight up and firmly spoke those words: "I'm going to win this community for Christ or die trying. If you feel any differently than that, you might as well pack up tonight and leave in the morning."

I was so excited to be linked up with a heart like his. I cried for joy—and stayed with him for thirteen years.

Strive for excellence
without extravagance.

We learned quickly at Skyline that people weren't drawn to the place because of its grand physical accoutrements—because we surely didn't have any. Our sanctuary was a five hundred-seat, box-like building with a steep roof and a steeple. There were no pews—only used wooden theater seats. No carpet, no stained glass windows, and no pipe organ. The parking lot was unpaved and gravel covered. The landscaping consisted of a small lawn on one side of the building and a few small plants for an attempt at greenery.

Skyline defied the "experts" who came to visit and check us out. People would often comment, "This really can't happen here." Pastor Butcher would smile at me and say, "I think we'll just keep working anyway." He was a man who could take the cold water thrown on his idea, heat it with enthusiasm, and use the steam to push ahead.

Pastor Butcher was sure of one thing. I heard him say many times, "The building doesn't have to be fancy, but it must be clean." Our wonderful, Norwegian custodian (in those days we had only one) was Daddy Berk. He loved those simple buildings with a passion. By 10:30 Monday morning, you could have eaten off the Sunday school building floors. Waxed and buffed, they lay proudly through the week, ready for any and all comers.

One Sunday morning during the offertory, Pastor Butcher leaned over to me and said, "I'll see you here at three this afternoon."

I replied, "I have a rehearsal for the evening service at three."

"Okay, make it two thirty then. There's a lightbulb out in the second chandelier on the left, and we have to change it before tonight. No burned-out bulbs in this church."

I held the ladder—and up he went. The sanctuary was simple, but perfect.

So why did so many people come? Well, it wasn't because of the beautiful carpet or the stained glass windows or the fancy pipe organ. Not that any of those things would be wrong, but those things focus on our physical comfort and aesthetic pleasure.

Pastor Butcher was adamant: "The world is asking only one question: 'Can you help me where I hurt?'" I believed him—and we did our best to fulfill his expectation and dream.

Success is another form of failure—
if we forget what our priorities are.

Skyline was right on the edge of Lemon Grove and Lomita Village. The community would soon grow, but for now, the only gathering areas were a small convenience store and our church grounds.

To say that the teen population was *tough* would be to seriously come in on the underside of the truth. They had grown into an unstructured *gang*—intent on drinking, drugs, and disaster. The nearby convenience store manager obtained an injunction to keep them off his property. That left Skyline as their only refuge.

They had no problem breaking into the church. More than one early Sunday morning, the pastors could be found cleaning up the nursery, which held the remains of the previous night's wild party. Some Sunday evening services were interrupted by drunken teens storming down the aisles singing, laughing, and shouting, "Hallelujah!"

Small and young as the church was, there still were some laymen who had strong ideas of what Skyline should be. Three of them approached Pastor Butcher with the ultimatum: "Either these kids go or we go. You choose. We don't want our children exposed to these kids or their lifestyle. Do like the store owner next door and seek a police injunction to keep them off this property or, unhappily, we will be forced to find somewhere else to attend."

It didn't take Pastor Butcher long to decide. "Men," he said, "I understand your concern. But here is mine. You and your families know the way to the cross. These young people do not have that knowledge, and God called me here to share that opportunity with them. If you make me choose between you and them, I will have to choose the teens."

One of the men said, "Then you know this church will never grow and be famous." To which Pastor Butcher replied, "Fame is not the issue; ministry is."

The men left, the teens stayed, and the church expanded. On my last Sunday at Skyline, there were over one thousand young people on the campus—at a church that cared enough to lead them toward the cross.

A leader with no followers is
just a man taking a walk.

"The best way to lead is by example," Pastor Butcher insisted. Actually, it was the only way to lead in the early days of Skyline. It was such a new church that there was hardly any lay constituency at all. The only way to get neighborhood men to help on the buildings and grounds was for the pastors to be there too, from dawn till dusk, beginning to end.

There was a time when a late-afternoon, torrential rain had clogged up the ditch intended for a sewer line. A non-church neighbor drove by and saw Pastor Butcher knee deep in red, adobe mud, trying desperately to clear out the trench by himself. Viewing the daunting task, the man stopped his car and yelled, "What do you think you're doing?"

"Cleaning this channel for the sewer pipe that's scheduled for tomorrow," Pastor Butcher yelled back.

"Well, you'll never get that done alone. Let me help," the stranger said. Together, those two men who had never met finished the job so the pipeline could be installed. If Pastor Butcher had not been willing to work in the mud, then that piece of work would never have been completed. More importantly, that man would never have found true peace of heart when he returned with his family to church on Sunday.

Early every Sunday morning, Pastor Butcher was alone, lighting up heaters in preparation for Sunday school. One morning, in the darkness that pervades the six o'clock hour, Pastor Butcher grabbed for a piece of brown crepe paper that had become entwined in the grate. As he pulled it free, he discovered that it was a full-grown snake. He shared that funny story (at least it was humorous by then) in the morning service, and he never had to do that task alone again. But that's how he got people involved—leadership by example.

The new Sunday school addition was built by "volunteer labor," Pastor Butcher and I being the only "weekday volunteers." We'd start at 5:30 every morning and then go home for lunch, ready to return at one so we could be pastors. Then on

Saturdays, the community men would join us, and together we constructed a real building—and a passionate church.

The second Sunday school building was 80 percent complete when it burned to the ground. But on Saturday, seventy-five of those neighborhood people gathered for the cleanup. The ladies fixed a sumptuous dinner, and then we all sang "How Great Thou Art." Tears streamed down the sooty cheeks of the men, while the ladies stood arm in arm as we lifted our hearts in fresh commitment to the one who called us to build His church in this place.

We all live under the same sky, but
we do not all have the same horizon.

My little tribe—wife, daughter, and me—suddenly seemed
very large when we moved into the parsonage with
Pastor Butcher and his family. The new little church barely
had enough money to pay me forty-five dollars a week, and
even that was "by faith." Buying or even renting a home
seemed next to impossible—until little eighteen-month-old
Julie Jo pulled off a big hunk of Pastor Butcher's dining room
wallpaper.

We learned that one of the church board members was
moving to Iowa, and his house would soon be on the market.

He needed thirty-five hundred dollars to cover his equity (please remember, this is more than a few years ago) and the house could be ours—including the furniture he didn't want to move out of state. He gave us two days to come up with the money.

Tuesday morning, Pastor Butcher sent me home from the office to get my bathing suit. "It looks like we're going swimming. Be ready."

We drove to Bonita, just south of Lemon Grove, to meet with Auntie Vi, a relative of Pastor Butcher's secretary. Auntie Vi spent most of her day in her swimming pool because her doctor said that was the best way to keep weight off her knees and ankles, which had become very painful. We swam and splashed long enough for me to turn into a giant prune.

Finally (after almost two hours of heavy moisturizing), we made it into her office. Pastor Butcher explained that we needed a house for me and my family, but some financial assistance was necessary.

"How much?" she asked.

"Thirty-five hundred dollars," was his hopeful reply.

"I can do that," she said. "And how do you plan to pay it back?" We, of course, had been hoping for a gift.

Neither of us had any money at all, so Pastor Butcher offered, "How about fifteen dollars a month?"

Auntie Vi thought for a moment, then said, "That won't even cover the interest. Oh, well," she continued, "I'll just pay that for you." And she wrote the check.

We went to Mr. Wallace's (name changed to protect the guilty) house that evening with the money. Astonished, he said, "I sold the house to someone else."

"But you promised it to us, and this money is *heaven sent*," Pastor Butcher pointed out. "Un-sell the house! You're not dealing with Skyline Church here, or with me. You're dealing with God!"

So, we got the house and lived happily there for five wonderful years.

A dream is not a thing possessed—
a dream possesses you.

Be sure you're committed to something bigger than yourself."
That was a motto we all lived by, day after day. I even had
it posted on my office wall for a while. To that, Pastor Butcher
added, "Give it all you've got. There's no turning back."

When he first arrived on the scene in Lemon Grove to
establish a spiritual "lighthouse" for the community, juvenile
delinquency was rampant. There was very little parental
control and even less police protection. His top priority was
correcting that problem with biblical truth. He organized
gatherings and events to draw those teenagers in and even

planned outings to encourage attendance and life-changing focus. After all, he had been an extremely successful youth pastor in Minneapolis. How different could San Diego teens be?

Fifty kids showed up for a party he planned. Musical chairs erupted into a melee. Chairs were knocked over in the ensuing brawl, as everyone went for the same seat when the music stopped. A game of drop-the-handkerchief turned into one fracas after another until the game ended, because the handkerchief disappeared. Pastor Butcher never did find his hankie.

When he borrowed a bus and took the young people to the beach, he noticed on the way home that there was some racket in the back. He turned on the interior lights and found that some of the couples were more interested in sexual exploration than in singing camp songs.

When asked how he responded, he simply said, "I turned off the lights."

Totally discouraged that night, he fell across his bed and wept. His wife came in and knelt beside him. "It looks like God answered your prayer," she whispered.

"What prayer was that?"

"Remember, you asked for a job too big—and it looks like God gave it to you."

"But, I don't have to do this. There are a lot of places I could go and serve better than this place."

"Jesus didn't have to go to the cross, either," she reminded him. "But he did, because he cared."

Pastor Butcher got up from that bed of discouragement and stepped back onto the battlefield. There was a job to be done—and together, he and Christ solved the delinquency problem of the community. And a church called Skyline rose up on the hill.

To see the seeds in an apple . . . that is reality.
To see the apples in a seed . . . that is vision.

Show me a man who has both feet
on the ground, and I'll show you a
man who can't get his pants on.

The well of creativity dries up only when we stop drawing
from it. It is deep and everlasting. We have to keep looking
for new concepts and new challenges.

Creativity is like finding the "pearl" in the center of the
onion. We have to keep pulling off layers until we finally get
there. There's nothing wrong with the outside sections—it's
just that the heart is superior.

At Skyline we were constantly looking for new ways to
express old truths—or rearranging old concepts in new
packages. There just had to be a fresher way.

Pastor Butcher insisted that we give ourselves to new vistas of excellence in every venture. For instance, the person who says, "I'm going to write a book someday if I can just get in the right mood and find enough time to do it right," will never bring the project to completion.

It's easy for anyone to say, "I'm out of ideas; I'm all dried up." But we dare not wait around until we have just the right feeling. Storing up our ideas so we can pour them out all at once will never work. The only way to be a writer is to write. A lot. And often.

Probably the greatest lock on creativity is to believe "I don't feel creative."

The principal mark of creativity is not perfection but originality. It is the opening of new frontiers.

Creativity is finding new things—or expressing old truths in new ways. It is making up new things—or rearranging old things in a new way.

All of life is a creative process.

So if you have writer's block, even sharpening your pencil will help, unless, of course, you're using a ballpoint pen.

Life without a dream is like
a hamburger without onions—
it just doesn't stick with you.

Pastor Butcher and I had been away for the afternoon, planning and evaluating different programs and possibilities for the church. I think I got pretty esoteric and he pulled me up short with this insight: "Now, Pastor Derric, if you want your dreams to come true, the first thing you will have to do is wake up."

We were watching men spread concrete as they poured it into the foundation for the new educational building at the church. It was quite fascinating. They wore high boots and moved constantly while they smoothed the mixture.

I commented to one of them that he seemed to be staying in constant motion. He replied, "When you're spreading concrete, you have to move. If you stand in one place too long, you might be there forever."

There is a time for careful planning and serious praying. But once that groundwork is laid, it's time to get up and move.

Pastor Butcher's formula was simple. First, you *visualize*—what needs to happen here? Keep asking, "What would we do if we knew we could not fail?" That's the greatest mind-stretcher I know.

Then you *verbalize*—you have to talk it out. Put the dream where you can see it. A dream really comes to one person, but partners bring a plan to fruition. Too many dreams lie dormant in the confines of a fertile mind and they erode . . . or rot.

Third, you *vitalize*—bring it to life. Money will always follow good ideas. Finding the right people with the proper perspective is the really important step.

And remember, success breeds success. Follow through on every facet of the dream. Your next venture depends on completing this one. Too many people are like fire trucks racing all around town—always smelling smoke but never finding fire.

You grade yourself by what you're going to do. People evaluate you by what you have already done. It's impossible to sell the idea of the *Queen Mary* if you've only ever built a rowboat.

Attempt the absurd
to achieve the impossible.

One day in a quiet, private conversation with Pastor Butcher, I mentioned that I was struggling to get a certain program to line up with the expected parameters, especially the budgetary safeguards and limitations. I never worried much about such things, but I understood that I was responsible to at least check it out. I was becoming agitated because I wasn't able to come up with the right answer. He looked at me and said, "Pastor Derric, stop trying to color inside the lines. Go ahead—*scribble*. You'll never get done what you want to do by trying to stay inside those parameters. Just stop trying to color inside the lines."

One constant deterrent to dreams is the concept we learn in school (and it's great for academics, but really wrong for life): "Find the right answer." As if there is only *one* right answer. For a lot of schoolwork, that may be true, but when it comes to real life, creativity demands that we get away from that one-answer point of view.

For instance, when we're three years old, we might learn that one plus one equals two. That is forever true, always immutable truth, never to change. Until we get a little older. Then we start to play around with numbers and realize that, when we put those two "ones" beside each other, one plus one becomes eleven. How much fun was it to tease your grandfather and say, "What's one plus one?" He'd say, "It's two," and you'd say, "No, it's eleven." Then you'd ask "How much is one plus one?" He'd say, "Eleven," and you'd say, "No, it's two!" until he got tired and said, "I don't want to play this game anymore."

Then one day you go to church for a wedding and you hear the preacher say, "Now the two shall become one." So now, one plus one equals one.

Then you learn what Jesus said about worship: "Where two of you are together and agree on anything in my name, I am right there in the midst of you." Now one plus one equals three.

Which one is the right answer? They're all right answers. It just depends what you're looking for. So stop trying to color inside the lines.

People may say that I've
been dreamin' a bit,
but I like what I'm believin',
and I'm not gonna quit.

While it's true that a dream comes to one person (never to a committee or a group), a dream must have *brain-company* to reach fulfillment. One person conceives it, and then a friend or a group formulates the plan to facilitate the dream.

A dream is intangible, but when two dream the same thing, it becomes concrete. Look at it this way. If you have a dollar and I have a dollar and we exchange those dollars, then we each still have a dollar. But if you have an idea and I have an idea and we exchange those, then we each have two ideas.

Because Pastor Butcher really believed the truth in Proverbs 27:17—"As iron sharpens iron, so one man sharpens another"—we spent considerable time together, verbally massaging concepts and bringing hopes to fruition.

Teams have always been important—Abbott had his Costello (imagine "Who's On First?" as a solo act); Rodgers needed to join with Hammerstein (otherwise there would have only been pretty poems and pointless melodies); there were two Wright brothers (like one for each wing); and don't forget David and Jonathan, Paul and Silas, and Peter and John.

An old country song puts it this way: "I was born a dreamer, but don't let me dream alone; we can make a dream that will last forever." Just as a flower bends toward the sun, so will a dream turn to a friend. That's when we move from "I think I can" to "we knew we could."

So, reach for a partner when you reach for your dreams, whatever they may be. Because you will grow from the reaching, while you learn from the trying—and you both win from the doing.

Faith sees the invisible,
believes the incredible, and
receives the impossible!

The New Sounds group was made up of sixteen great college singers and instrumentalists. I was desperate to take them on tour to the foreign mission field. Skyline Church needed an awakening to stimulate its missions program because the church was comprised of new believers who had neither compassion nor passion for needs on other continents. I was sure that if I could get these collegians to South America and let them come back to express their eyewitness testimonies, the situation would be remedied.

We scheduled a musical missionary opportunity of fifteen days through Ecuador and Colombia, and I knew the schedule would be extremely intense. We would not be on a sightseeing trip. So I told Pastor Butcher, "I've got to find a way to get money to fly these people down there."

He said, "Can't they raise the money?"

"No, I don't *want* them to raise the money. The schedule is going to be so hard that I don't want anybody backing out. My big fear would be that one of the singers might say, 'I'm really tired, I don't feel like going today. I paid for this trip. I'm staying in bed.' So I've got to pay for the trip. I've got to *own* their time, so I can say, 'No, you're not staying in bed. We'll rest when we get home or to heaven, whichever comes first.'"

We were getting close to the time of leaving on the tour and, as of yet, no funding had miraculously appeared—I *had* to buy the tickets. Talking to Pastor Butcher, I said, "I don't know how, but we've got to go."

He replied, "So what will you do, mortgage your house?"

"That's a great idea!" So I did. I mortgaged the house and bought the tickets for the singers, a photographer, and me—all eighteen of us. We did ninety-eight performances during that fifteen-day tour—inhuman, I know, but that's why I needed to "own them."

We returned to Miami from Medellin and traveled for two weeks across America singing, taking offerings, and selling records, so I could buy my house back.

What difference did that trip make? From the New Sounds came pastors, youth ministers, and missionaries—not to mention a fire for missions that still glows in the congregation.

Don't give God instructions; just
show up for duty.

Here is a mind-expanding theory from Pastor Butcher: "If we
can explain how we did it, then God didn't do it. Now, that
doesn't mean he didn't bless it. It just means he didn't do it."

He went on: "If we try to document all of our programs
and innovations so someone can replicate them somewhere
else, it's really a waste of time. So much of what happened
here is not transferable." Those of us who were watching
Skyline blossom lived in a whirlwind of the unexplained.

Over and over we met them—leaders from other churches
and denominations who came and asked, "How in the world do

you do this, and in this place?" They were referring to our poor little sanctuary, which only seated five hundred fifty people, and our non-landscaped property that didn't even have a paved parking lot.

One man mumbled through his amazement, "What you do is really quite unexplainable. Then when I see where you do it—it is miraculous. No one could have done that in his own power. It could only happen one way. God made Skyline."

That kind of attitude didn't just keep us on our toes; it drove us to our knees. It was God who gave the dream. He just asked us to work on it. Our whole way of thinking became "Not of works, lest any man should boast." Pastor Butcher saw to it that God got the credit. We may have done some work on his project, but he deserved the acclaim.

There was no room for the "diva" lifestyle or attitude, no place for cocky back-slapping, no singing, "How great I am, how great I am."

Remember the story about two men fishing? One man was experienced and acting as the teacher, while the other man was just a beginner. Every time the teacher caught a big fish, he put it in his ice chest to keep it fresh. But the student threw all the big fish back into the pond. When the teacher asked why, the inexperienced fisherman replied, "I only have a small frying pan."

Never limit what God can do by what you think you can do.

You must invest in leaders—
that's what Jesus did.

I had been serving happily in my position as high school youth pastor for almost a year when Pastor Butcher invited me to his office—always a time of exhilaration for me. He told me he appreciated the job I was doing with the teens and expressed gratitude for the obvious growth in the program. Then he stunned me by asking, "Where's your football captain?"

"I beg your pardon," I squeaked out. "We don't have a football captain."

"I can tell that by looking at the boys in the class. You can't have a bona fide youth program in San Diego County without a football captain."

"And how do I do that?"

He smiled and suggested, "Ask next Sunday in class if anyone goes to school with an unsaved, unchurched football captain."

I did, and every hand in the place went up. It seemed that every football captain was unsaved and unchurched. It must have been like a job description.

I set up a "burger" appointment with Russ, newly selected captain of the Grossmont High School football team. We met to talk about college scholarships, and then I asked if he went to church anywhere.

"Nope," he replied.

"Why not?"

"Nobody ever asked me."

"Well, I'm asking you. You need to come to Skyline. You'll love it. Besides, you have a hole in your soul." He looked at his foot. "Not that sole, the one inside you."

We ended up that afternoon in my office, and Russ gave his life to Christ. What a magnet he was, drawing other teens to the church and the cross.

Pastor Butcher's mandate for leadership was that we should go for those who can most influence others. Win the football captain and you get the homecoming queen, the head cheerleader, the linebacker, the split end, and the water boy.

Win the water boy, and you get the water boy. Now, that's not to say the football captain's soul is of greater importance, but his influence is. Russ went on to be a pastor and high school mentor and coach; he is still a magnet for Christ.

Only God can make flowers
and trees; I am in charge
of seeds and weeds.

Often, ministry staff people from other churches would visit us at Skyline hoping for special insights and magical concepts to grow their congregations. Many of them would eventually get around to asking questions about the so-called hallmark of leadership success: "How many outstanding people have you mentored into the marketplace?" Or, "How many famous people hold their church membership in Skyline?"

Pastor Butcher's response was always the same: "We don't deal in *stars* here. I choose not to show you those successes. Judge us rather by the *servants* who have gone from this place."

He would talk about Dorothy, a single mother of three who cleaned the restrooms at Grossmont Hospital to support her family. Five days a week she worked there, and on her day off, she came by Skyline voluntarily to do the same for us. Often, through tears of gratitude, he would exclaim, "And do you know what? We have the cleanest toilets in San Diego County." There was something else about Dorothy. Based on her income, she gave more money to missions than anyone else in the church. That's being a servant.

Then there was Mac, a service station manager who was the self-appointed head of ushers and a brilliant stage manager who cared for every detail.

No one could forget Ed, who put himself in charge of the parking lots and songbooks when there was no one else to do it.

Where's the servanthood in that? None of them was ever asked to do it. They didn't receive acclaim or commendation; it was a job to be done, and they did it for the Lord.

We will be remembered more for our kindnesses than our accomplishments, for our generosity than our riches, and for our service than our successes.

People are like envelopes—those stamped IMPORTANT seldom are.

Commit yourself to a dream
that will take your breath away.

The high school ministry had leveled off. We were stuck at about one hundred twenty-five students every Sunday morning for our class meeting. Something had to be done to break away from this attendance plaza of mediocrity. Somehow the passion for outreach was sorely absent. We were just happy to be together—kind of a "comfort club for the saints."

With Pastor Butcher's blessing, we determined to have a serious contest to bring in new students to the class— a king or queen of Skyline contest determined solely by who brought the most first-timers. Then came the dilemma: What would be the prize for the king or queen?

When Pastor Butcher first quizzed me about the award, I mumbled something about a pen and pencil set or a camera. He looked at me and said, "Pastor Derric, no one will win that prize. They'll just get it. What would a high school student want more than anything in the world?"

I grinned. "A car."

"Good idea. Give away a car!"

"You've got to be kidding," I stammered in rebuttal. "This church can barely pay my salary. How will I get a car to give away?"

"I don't know. But it was your idea. Go for it."

I went to see the sales manager at the Lemon Grove Plymouth dealership, hoping he'd give me one. "I don't need much of a car—just some clunker that can run off the church property on its own power. What happens after it turns the corner is not my problem."

He had no cars like that and wouldn't have them on his lot if he did. "I'll check back in a couple of days, just in case," I said.

I went to El Cajon to a really cheapo car lot. They had my car . . . for five hundred dollars. But please remember, I'm penniless. Friday morning I went back to the Plymouth guy. Still no luck there, but he said, "I really appreciate what your youth program has done for my daughter. Let me buy the El Cajon car for you!" He gave me a check for five hundred dollars.

In El Cajon the dealer said, "Okay, I'm going to let you have this car for three hundred fifty dollars." And I've got a U-Haul trailer friend who will paint it bright orange for you."

You should have seen the expressions on those teens' faces when I drove onto the parking lot and said, "Whoever brings the most visitors in the next four Sundays *gets this car*!"

Gary Beebe won by bringing eighty-eight first-time visitors that month. And that just scratched the surface of the more than twelve hundred new people who came to check us out . . . and give us a chance to touch their lives.

We are all producers—some make good, others make trouble, and still others make excuses.

No one was further from being a "numbers worshiper" than Pastor Butcher. He had no competitive agenda when it came to other churches. Size mattered only in relation to ministry measurement.

"It's important," he would say, "that we maintain an edge of consistency. How will we know if what we are doing will really matter in the lives of people around us? Every shepherd counts his flock." Remember the story in Luke 15 of the ninety-nine sheep who were safely tucked in for the night when the good shepherd realized one was missing? How would he have known that if he didn't keep track of the number?

"So I am concerned with how many we have in the youth group, the music ministry, and the prayer partners. Statistics are souls. If we can't count them, we're not reaching them."

"But how do you counter the argument that 'quality is more important than quantity'?" I asked. "I hear that all the time."

"Well," he answered, smiling, "I would say that the only people who contend that numbers don't count are the people who don't have any numbers to count. Besides, you have a better chance at quality if you have quantity. Without quantity, where do you get the quality people?"

For us at Skyline, the stated purpose was always "Where can we do the greatest good for the most people in the least amount of time?"

It all revolves around potential. When it's all said and done, we will be judged not by what we did, but by what we could have done . . . and didn't.

Did you realize that a cloud is 96 percent water and a watermelon is 93 percent water? That rolling-on-the-ground piece of fruit missed soaring through the sky as a high-flying cloud by just 3 percent! So there you have it—reach for the sky.

Never let the purse strings tie
up your heart strings.

Absolutely and without a doubt, some of the best times of
my life were those early days at Skyline when we had no
money available for projects and outreach. Actually, we had a
printed budget; we just had no money *to* budget. We had two
options: (1) sit around and wait for money or (2) claim our
dreams by faith without "provided money."

At such times, Pastor Butcher felt we needed a plan of
action. First, he would ask, "What do we *need* to do?" The key
word is *need*, not *want*. Second, "How much will it cost?" And
third, "Where do we get the money?" The typical "budgeteer"

reverses those questions: (1) How much money do we have, (2) how shall we disperse it, and (3) how little can we do and still get by?

How we love to take financial pledges and then sing "Faith Is the Victory." Pastor Butcher's feeling was that stewardship is a virtue, but it's not necessarily faith—and who wants to sing "Stewardship Is the Victory"?

The question is often asked, "Can we afford to do that?" A better question is, "Can we afford *not* to do that?" If we're not careful, "budget" becomes a piece of paper that is used to limit the power of God.

Remember the story in John 6 concerning the feeding of the five thousand. Jesus took Philip aside—Philip being the disciple who thought nothing should be done for the first time—and asked, "How shall we feed these people?" Philip was aghast, and said, "It can't be done. We don't have enough money to feed this crowd. Even if we did, there is no place to secure the food." Philip evaluated the solution to the hunger problem on the basis of his personal resources.

But Jesus didn't ask, "How shall *you* feed these people?" because Philip couldn't. Nor did he ask, "How shall *I* feed these people?" because Jesus wouldn't. Notice the pronoun he used: "How shall *we* feed these people?"

When we look at each other around a boardroom table, we may rightly say, "We can't do it." But when we factor the divine *we* into the equation, all things are possible.

We must do more than convert the
will; we must cultivate the taste.

Traditionally, in the early days of Skyline, every Sunday
evening service began with the high school youth choir
singing as they processed down the aisles. Right on the dot at
seven, (Pastor Butcher always said that you never penalize the
people who come on time) the piano and organ would start to
play, and the teenagers would start to march down the aisles
vocalizing to the tune of "Every Step I Take, I Take with Jesus."

It was interesting, if not an outright joy, to watch the
congregation scatter to find seats. Ours was a very fellowship-
oriented church. We did not have a big foyer, so before service

time, people would stand in the aisles talking to one another.

But when the music started and the students came quickly down those aisles on the way to the platform, folks hurried to their seats. The reason is that the kids had been instructed, "Move straight through. Don't stop for anything, short of knocking someone down. You have to get to the platform. This entrance is timed."

We always had unique ways of getting on stage. Sometimes we'd serpentine the choir, crisscrossing like a marching band. Or we'd spread out the singers in different positions when they arrived on the platform. Or they'd move in "lock step" onto risers. People came early to see what would be next.

One time I mentioned to Pastor Butcher, "It's just amazing how people scatter when the choir starts down the aisles."

He replied, "You've just uncovered a great concept of leadership. You've seen it work, so now understand it. You're in control when people do what you want them to do without your telling them to do it. In this case you want them to sit down so we can start the service on time. Now, there are a couple of ways we can accomplish that. You can get up in front and say, 'Everybody, please take a seat. We're beginning to sing the first verse of this song.' But nobody will. They'll finish their sentence or keep exchanging their recipes, or whatever other personal talk they're engaged in. But send those teenagers purposefully down the aisle, and there's nothing else for the people to do except get out of the way.

"If they only sit down when you beg, plead, or threaten, you're not in control. You're just directing traffic."

Not all the hammerheads
are in the water!

The church was growing and God was blessing—or so it seemed to us! But from somewhere (I think out of the pit) there rose up a band of those cautionary people who always want to play it safe—to a fault.

I asked Pastor Butcher, "Where do these people come from?"

"Which people?"

"The ones who think nothing should be done for the first time."

"Be patient with them; they'll come around," he assured me.

"But these people have their spiritual transmission in park, and they want to leave it there," I complained. Usually they were the people who had transferred to Skyline somewhat unhappily from other congregations. Then they wanted to make our church like theirs. "We don't like it when it changes!" was more than a watchword. It became their battle cry!

Eventually (and unfortunately), some of those individuals were elected to our board of stewards and trustees. That was the first time in the early years we had any yammering or complaining about the mission and program of the church. There were two men in particular who would gripe and grumble about everything—from the phone bill to the air conditioning in the office to the microphones on the platform.

After one rather tense and long board meeting, Pastor Butcher had had enough. As the two members were leaving the building to get to their cars, he said to them, "Let me walk with you. I think we should talk."

I was going the same direction, so I pulled another man with me to walk parallel to them. "Don't talk; just walk. I really want to see how Pastor Butcher handles this situation." Eavesdropping through the parking lot, I heard Pastor Butcher say, "Gentlemen, no one says you have to like it here. But if you don't like it here, don't *stay* here and don't like it. Go somewhere else and don't like it here. I really don't want you to leave, but please, don't stay and be unhappy."

I watched them shake hands and all drive away. The men stayed in the church with whole new attitudes and became great members of the ministry team.

I asked Pastor Butcher the next morning about the confrontation. He smiled and said, "No matter what, Pastor Derric, let the church roll on! That's paramount."

I'm *nobody*, telling *everybody* about
somebody who can save *anybody*.

Pastor Butcher loved encouraging people to share their faith verbally and publicly, whether it was their newfound understanding or cultured in years of experience. Often, believers were given the opportunity to share how God's grace had been manifest in their lives lately.

When Pastor Butcher told me there would be a "Praisefest" on Thanksgiving morning from 8:30 until 11:30, I made some grand comment like "You're crazy! No one will come to church at that time on that morning." He shook his head and said, "Just wait and see."

The sanctuary was *packed* with standing room only as people waited for an opportunity to reveal what God had done in their lives. The service became an annual tradition. Thanksgiving morning was divided into fifteen-minute sections, with a well-defined theme for each segment—parents of this year's newborns, members who had joined the church this year, people married this year, and of course, charter members who had watched the church grow and expand since its inception.

Over and over again, people's hearts overflowed with praise and joy and commitment. I'll never forget Katherine standing for her allotted minute, not saying a word, just weeping over the goodness of God—then she sat down. The next year, she brought Pastor Butcher a poem for him to read while she stood, not saying a word. It was a simple rhyme with profound significance: "Tears are My Testimony."

Or Donald, facing serious cancer surgery, declaring, "I know what I believe; now I get to see if I *believe* what I know."

The testimony groupings were always punctuated with appropriate choir presentations. The choir had to be at church by 7:45 for warm up and platform placement. No one ever missed the morning.

Never underestimate the power of advertising by word of mouth. A codfish lays ten thousand eggs a day, but it's done silently. A hen lays one egg a day and cackles about it. Nobody eats codfish eggs, but nearly everybody eats chicken eggs.

He who has a thing to sell
And goes and whispers in a well,
Is not so apt to get the dollars
As he who climbs a tree and hollers.

In your witness don't brag, don't nag, don't lag, and don't sag.

You cannot control the length of your life . . .
But you can control the width and depth.

A good idea is a very dangerous
thing—if it's the only one you have.

thinking ahead

It was the first of November, and I went into Pastor Butcher's office to share all the details of the coming Christmas cantata "Down the Stairway of Stars." I had the lighting effects, sound requirements, and budget proposals all neatly organized for his perusal and permission.

He glanced at my lists briefly and then looked up at me before saying, "I know the Christmas presentation will be great, because you're doing it. But what's your encore?"

"You mean an extra song at the end? We'll be lucky to get all the scheduled material memorized."

"No, I mean what's next? What's your encore? Before the downbeat on Christmas, I want to know your theme and some of the songs for Easter."

"Easter? I don't have Jesus out of the manger yet, and you want him off the cross and out of the tomb?"

"That's right. The most important choir rehearsal you'll have is the Thursday night right after the Christmas production is over. If you're working on just one thing at a time, fatigue sets in. You get tired, or maybe sickly and run down, and the choir sags into adrenalin depletion. To maintain momentum, you've got to be always working on the next project. So, what's your encore?"

Creativity is like a bicycle ride. To be working on one project at a time is the same as moving a one-pedaled bike uphill. Push that one pedal down and then you spend most of the rest of your time sticking your foot under the broken pedal to pull it back up again so you can shove it down to keep going forward. Trouble is, you lose all your forward thrust—and you are probably ready to fall off.

Two concepts are like two pedals—not just nice, but necessary. They keep everyone motivated and thinking ahead. They instill excitement and encourage inspiration.

It's a clarion call to excellence: "What's your encore?"

Creativity without discipline is like an octopus on roller skates. There is plenty of movement, but you never know if it's going to be forward, backward, or sideways.

We all have to answer to someone sometime. When we are in our teens, we can't wait to get out of the house and on our own. Find a job and we discover there's an over-achieving boss who expects that same work ethic out of us. Get married and the husband wears the pants in the family, while the wife provides the suspenders. When do we get the chance to say with feeling, "I am my own boss"? Actually, never! We always have to answer to someone.

The Skyline Chorale had suffered an embarrassing moment during an evening production when the lights wouldn't come on until we sang. The problem was that we couldn't sing until the lights came on. There were so many cords and cables strung out across the platform that I dared not walk to the lighting technician with instructions. Instead, I crawled in the dark to where he was sitting and gave the command for blue lights. They came up as I was still moving quickly across the stage on my hands and knees.

Obviously we either would never use lights or never use music again. Wisely, the Skyline Chorale chose to work hard and forgo the holding of books. That wonderful group of talented singers made a commitment with me to memorize *all* our music, always. It was like a spiritual thing—never hold music in a service again.

When Pastor Butcher's mother passed away, the Skyline Chorale was scheduled to sing at the funeral. He took me aside and explained that while she was taking her last breaths, the family stood around her bed and sang her favorite song about heaven, "My Home Sweet Home."

"I want the choir to sing that this afternoon. I know you don't have that song in your repertoire, but you'll find it on page 168 of our evening hymnal."

"But the chorale has a commitment . . ."

He interrupted. "I understand that. You want to do everything from memory, but this is special. I want you to use the music and lead them in that song. If you need a reason why, here it is: *Because I said so*."

That was enough for me!

Patience is keeping cool as a
cucumber while the rest of
the world is going bananas.

T he organ will be here longer than you will."

That statement marked my first lesson in patience. I am an
impetuous person by nature—move now or forever be stuck. I
have always been prone to giving the correct answer *immediately*
to any situation or question when I'm sure I'm right—in those
days that meant "always."

The church was ready to purchase an organ. We had
one that had been donated because the people didn't use it
anymore. When you heard it, you knew exactly why. But that
musical piece of furniture did enough to whet the appetite of

the Skyline Church board, bringing some understanding of instrumental necessity.

I, of course, knew exactly what kind of organ we needed, where to get it, and precisely how much it would cost. "Let's move *now*—before someone changes his mind." Then, that ugly word that every dreamer detests entered into the equation—*committee*. At our first meeting, I was appalled to learn that these individuals would make the decision on the size, sound, and monetary value of the purchase.

"But, Pastor Butcher, none of these people are even musical, let alone a musician. On what basis will they make their decision? It just seems wrong. Who do they think they are? We just need to move on and get what we think is best for us."

"Define *us*," Pastor Butcher countered.

"Well, you and me."

"Pastor Derric, this church is much more and a lot bigger than *us*. It's about people joining together in a journey of faith. They need to express their feelings about our direction."

And then he let it fly—words I had never thought of before: "The organ will be here a lot longer than you and I will. Let them have their voice."

Patience is trusting God more than trusting self. Get in line and watch him work. It can be so easy to be insistent on the Burger King mantra—have it your way—that we miss the bigger picture of what God has in mind. Don't be guilty of winning the battle but losing the war.

Sometimes you have to weigh
the votes—not just count them.

Some people have an ego that is guarded by an eggshell: fragile, tender, and easily bruised. Count me as one of those. I've always tried to be a people pleaser, often to a fault. The worst thing I can ever face is the feeling that someone is unhappy with me or what I've done—or dream to do.

In the early days of Skyline, the denomination had mandated that the full-time pastoral staff be voted on annually. The process was simple. While members gathered in a congregational meeting in the sanctuary, the pastors with their families retired to a waiting room (torture chamber to me), and the chairman of the board took over. Ballots were distributed to every member, who then voted on each pastor separately. The ballot contained just two boxes: *change* and *no change*. Wow, take your pick.

Pastor Butcher would smile and say, "Pastor Derric, everything will be fine. You'll see. Relax." *Relax* . . . ha! That was like hanging a "Keep Cool" sign in the middle of hell—nice sentiment, but totally impractical.

"Easy for you to say," I would respond every year. "You've never received a negative vote in your life. Everybody loves you. I'm a different story."

But finally we were called back into the sanctuary. It was always the same—a unanimous vote for *no change*. We were safely ministering for one more year.

Like I said, it was always the same, except for one year. Two *change* votes were cast after my name. I was ready to quit. Pastor Butcher tried to calm me down. "Two out of six hundred votes are hardly overwhelming. Besides, let me check and find out who those people were. If it is the chairman of the board and the financial secretary, that's a lot different than two unhappy grandmothers ganging up on you."

And guess what? It *was* two grandmothers who felt slighted when their two granddaughters didn't make it into the high school chapel choir. They wanted to teach me a lesson about my audition process being too hard.

Pastor Butcher was right—again. "You must know the criticizer before you can evaluate the criticism."

Success without a successor
is a failure.

It was time for a change of focus in my ministry. I had started out with Pastor Butcher as a high school youth pastor—with music thrown in later—and loved every minute of it.

Eventually, my heart seemed to be drawing me toward deeper ministry and mentoring. I talked with Pastor Butcher about moving my "youth" energies toward the potential of a college ministry. To that point we had shipped our high school graduates off to a number of fine colleges, but it seemed that many of them would go away and lose their passion and purpose for evangelism and outreach.

"Could we keep some of these movers and shakers at home for college by starting a ministry for them here?" was my first question for the pastor. "I'd love to work with them in the three areas of your *mission* in life (what you are going to do), your *master* in life (who you will do it for), and your *mate* in life (who you will do it with).

He smiled and said, "You think you want to move from high school ministry to college students. But when you see those hundreds of teens and hear them singing while you are meeting with seventeen collegians in the kitchen of the fellowship hall after a Saturday night fish fry, you'll miss it. So here's the deal. You find your own person to pass the torch to."

"But surely, you know someone," I countered.

"Not to take your place, I don't. You pick your own replacement. It will be much better that way."

In November at the national Wesleyan Youth Convention in Louisville, Kentucky, it fell into place. I was leading the choir there, Otis Skillings was at the piano, and Pastor Butcher was speaking. Someone came to me and said, "There's a guy here you should meet. I think you guys are peas in a pod."

We walked down the hall and there was Jimmy Johnson—effervescent, charismatic, loud, and funny—just right for "my" high school ministry. He came to us from Alabama, and together we shared great years in joined ministry. I loved having him at Skyline—because he was my choice. I chose my successor.

Ministry happens whenever
divine resources meet human
needs through loving hearts
for the glory of God.

At staff coffee one Monday morning, Pastor Butcher suspended our casual conversation with this gentle illustration.

"Yesterday morning after the eleven o'clock service, while we were greeting our people, I felt a tug at my coat. I turned around to see who was there. Apparently, no one. I thought I had been mistaken, so I resumed the greetings.

"Then, the tug again. This time I turned and looked down. It was little Amy." She was the staff favorite—four years old, bright-eyed, and with a smile that lit up the whole world.

"I knelt down beside her," Pastor Butcher continued. "She didn't say a word, just held out her little finger to me. It was brightly wrapped in a Mickey Mouse Band-Aid. I peeled the bandage off and there was a little cut on the tip of her pinky. I held it close, kissed it gently, and wrapped the Band-Aid around it again. We smiled at each other, and she ran to find her mommy.

"Now boys," he said speaking to us on his staff, "everything you need to know about ministry and pastoral theology is right there.

"Number 1: She wasn't afraid of me.

"Number 2: She knew I would care.

"Number 3: She knew I would do something about it."

And I thought, *I could have passed two out of three on that test. I'm smart enough to kneel down next to Amy. And I'm sensitive enough to pull the bandage off. But to kiss the cut—to help her where she hurt—I'm not sure I ever would have thought of that on my own.*

But I always have after that!

Empathy is putting *your* pain in *my* heart.

It was four days before Christmas. Pastor Butcher was in downtown San Diego singing at a seasonal celebration, when his son came by my house and told me of a sudden, unexpected death in our church family. It was my responsibility to get there and do what comforting I could until Pastor Butcher would arrive.

The house was beautifully decorated with multicolored lights twinkling on a softly flocked, white Christmas tree. Now, this was my first crack at the comfort business—and I was nervous. So I quoted all the scriptures I knew about the subject of solace (some of them twice) to console the people, trying to remove the spirit of agitation while providing some semblance of peaceful repose. We talked about assurance and prospect and how wonderful heaven must be. The conversation was *spiritual*, but *empty*.

Finally the pastor came (about midnight I recall) and said to the wife of the grieving household, "When I first heard your father had died, I thought I needed to leave the platform and hurry to you. But then I remembered two things: (1) I did have an obligation to the people I was with and (2) we knew by example and testimony where your father was. So I finished there and here I am. We don't need to talk much tonight, do we? Your father is in heaven and far better off than we are. But it is lonely for us who have been left here without him, isn't it? I know how you feel, because I lost my mother at Thanksgiving a year ago. So I just came by to cry with you for a while."

And he sat down on the sofa with the bereaved daughter, held her hand for twenty minutes, and quietly wept with her, while the rest of us watched. Then he asked if all the arrangements had been taken care of and was there anything else he could do? Assured that everything was fine, he offered a brief, heartfelt prayer and left.

He used to say, "We need to stop spelling ministry with a capital 'M.' The real impact on people happens when ministry is spelled with a small 'm.'" That night, I got it.

And I never forgot his words, "*I know how you feel.*" That is ministry distilled.

When it comes to ministry,
we are not manufacturers—
we are distributors.

I n this time of megachurches, famous pastors, best-selling authors, and TV personalities, there always seems to be a rush to see who can work their way to the top of the mountain and be the most acclaimed. But real ministry is like an inverted pyramid—it's not about reaching the peak and being the most acclaimed and famous, but about working your way to the base of the pyramid and touching people where they live and hurt.

Pastor Butcher always had time for people who needed him, regardless of whether they could do anything for him in return. Case in point—everyone at Skyline remembers Tony, a Tijuana soul-winner who came around the church just for company. I always felt that Pastor Butcher needed to put a sign on his desk that read "If you have nothing to do, please don't do it here." But that attitude was far from being the attitude of Pastor Butcher's heart.

Tony would stop by at the most awkward times and say in his enthusiastic Mexican accent, "Pastor Butcher, come to the altar and pray with me." Off they would go, leaving sometimes a pile of work to be completed later in the evening. When the prayer time was over, you could count on Tony to plead, "Pastor Butcher, sing for me. Sing "How Great You Are." Pastor Butcher would move to the piano on the platform and start to sing in that truly great voice of his, "How Great Thou Art," while Tony sat on the front pew, weeping until his shirt was wet with praise-full tears.

"I didn't think you had time for that," I admonished him.

"Pastor Derric, there's always time for the Tonys. Don't ever forget that."

Pastor Butcher's wonderful wife and partner passed into her eternal reward in 1988. I remember her well, not because she was a great singer or polished pianist. She was neither. She did have a gift for teaching God's Word. But I really remember her because she cared—cared about a young pastor coming onto the staff, cared enough to be constantly encouraging, cared enough to always offer another chance to make it better.

It wasn't her up-reach or even her out-reach that impressed me. It was her down-reach. I think her daughter, Sharon Butcher Westfall, summed up her mother's life best with her words at the memorial service: "Mom, when people say I've grown up to look and act like you, I smile in my heart because that means I grew up to be exactly what I wanted to be."

If you try to improve another person
by setting a good example, then you
are really improving two people.

When visiting staff members from other churches would come to Skyline, Pastor Butcher would sometimes single one out and ask, "What's your ministry?"

The response would usually run the full course: "Well, I direct the music ministry as well as the youth and do some visitation," or "The children's ministry and music are my responsibility," or "I serve as the chief financial officer of my church."

I enjoyed the smile on Pastor Butcher's face when he gently responded, "No, that's not your ministry. That's your job description. If you don't do that, you don't get paid. It's what you do *off* the platform or *away* from your desk that defines your ministry."

There was always a look of shock, disbelief, irritation, or even anger. "Who is this man to challenge me and my concept of ministry?" was the question to be read on every face.

He would go on. "For the people in your church—the dentist who teaches Sunday school, the bank teller who sings in the choir, or the gas station manager who ushers—for those people, that's ministry, because those things stretch them from daily tasks in service for the Savior.

"You are very fortunate to make your living in a ministry venue, but that in itself does not qualify as 'ministry.' My focus question for all of us is, 'What do we do for Jesus and the people he cares about while we're away from the public platform?'

"Now, that is certainly *not* to negate your platform service or personality. In fact, you'd better be really good on the platform or in your position, or no one will care who you are or what you think off the platform and in private settings.

"We need to be very aware of personal extension and involvement in people's lives. That's where the sacrifice of comfort and time to mentor and inspire come into the picture. Ministry, properly speaking, always involves doing something personal for Christ at a personal cost to yourself—and by your own choice.

"Because that's what Paul meant when he wrote, 'What you've heard from me, commit to faithful men, who shall be able to teach others also,' and we should do that by careful modeling."

If you think you're too small to
have an impact, try going to
bed with a mosquito.

Here is a great Pastor Butcher observation: "The greatest
gift you will ever have is not the gift of performance. (By
performance, I mean 'actively using what God gave you.')
There is a gift that is much scarcer, something finer by far
than ability. It is the ability to recognize ability. Your greatest
talent will be finding the gifts God has given to others and
then helping them use their skills to the maximum."

You don't need to have great personal talent in every area
of life. Your real job is to be a "gift-finder." Remember what
the apostle Paul wrote in 1 Corinthians 7:7, "I wish that all

men were as I am. But each man has his own gift from God." Identify the people who have specific gifts and talents and provide the opportunity, equipment, and encouragement for them to dream, grow and succeed.

Take Toby Foster, for instance. I met him while he was still a junior high student. He used my backyard tool shed to repair all sorts of electrical appliances and doodads. I shopped with him and bought all his first knobs. Ultimately, he designed and built a recording studio at the church, then went on to great success and fame in Hollywood and Chicago as a premier recording engineer. I couldn't do it myself; it was way past my own abilities and understanding. But I gave him the push.

And there was Alden Butcher, the first PK at Skyline (yep, Pastor Butcher's firstborn). Even as a teen, he showed brilliant promise as an artist, set designer, and photographer. We collaborated on a number of projects before he went on to become a famous media producer.

Dave Johnson was an intuitive genius in the area of sound and lights. He was another man in that line who didn't believe the word *impossible*, which led him into a brilliant career in the field of light design.

Bob Clark was another incredible sound tech, even in his high school years. He designed a sound board for The Re'Generation (a traveling group) that I couldn't dare to sit behind. He is in Nashville today, a primo studio engineer who is always in demand.

I'll never forget Ron Coker, a gregarious teen who was his high school class president in his freshman, sophomore, junior, and senior years. Then he started Re'Generation, moved to Nashville, where he became vice president of development, and today has become a "mover-shaker-influencer" in the music and print industries.

They did what I could never do; but I was there at their beginnings.

Experience is something you don't
get until just after you needed it.

This is a physical object lesson Pastor Butcher taught me the hard way. Actually, I think it was easy for him to teach— just hard for me to learn. It all happened at a Monday night board meeting. Pastor Butcher was at the head of the table and always had me sit at his left (so he could "get at me," I found out later).

We were discussing the potential uses of the now empty parsonage where Pastor, Mrs. Butcher, and their three children had lived for ten years. The lovely building was situated conveniently on the edge of the church property, and since the

Butcher family was moving to a private home in Lemon Grove, we needed to establish another use for the structure.

Now, remember that I'm the collegian pastor, so my first priority is for my people and program. This building consisted of a large living room where we could easily seat more than a hundred students for gatherings, when it was not being used as a quiet, secluded study hall. It had a vaulted wood ceiling, a charming fireplace, room for my office, and space for my secretary. The garage could be set up as a recreation room with ping-pong and pool tables, isolating noise in the garage so that study could go on in the collegian lounge. We would develop a library there containing books that would be unavailable at the San Diego State University property—Bible dictionaries, encyclopedias, commentaries, and other volumes to assist the committed Christian collegian on his or her spiritual journey.

If you think I had spent a lot of time working all this out, you're right—time *and* prayer. So it was no small disaster when some of the board members had "other ideas." They couldn't do that to me and mine.

One offered the thought that the junior high ministry should take over this beautiful building. I wanted to shout, "Are you crazy? They'll tear it up!" But before I got to the word *crazy*, I felt a sharp kick to my shin—sharp enough to stop my words as I sucked in breath. Then someone else trashed that concept, so I didn't have to.

"What a great spot for the children's ministry," was another wacko idea. Before I could utter a word (he heard my preparatory breath), Pastor Butcher gave me another shot to the shins.

Ultimately (and without much discussion), the facility went to the collegians, and we enjoyed its focus for five years. Pastor Butcher taught me well that night: "Never speak to an issue that is obviously going your way. Remember Barney Fife—save your bullets for the biggies."

Like a grove of redwood trees,
the closer we stand, the
stronger we are.

We ride and build on each other's successes," Pastor Butcher
said. "Ministry is not a competition. The better you do, the
better we all look. So let's find ways to help and support one
another. We have no Lone Rangers on this staff. The ground is
level here. We will learn to lean on one another."

Pastor Butcher made sure that we built an affinity established
on a bond of warmth. He never let us underestimate the power
of association and friendly fellowship. We had staff coffee for
twenty minutes every morning beginning at 10:00. If you
were on property, you were required to attend. Those coffee

times never had anything to do with business, calendars, or problems. It was all about camaraderie.

Then there was staff prayer time every Tuesday morning from 7:30 till 9:00. So when the official staff meeting for work and decisions came around every Thursday from 11:30 till 1:00, all the melting of soul and melding of spirit in the social and spiritual times made ministry matters easy to transact.

It is imperative here to note that nobody was unimportant on the staff, including secretaries and custodians. They were always included and esteemed for who they were and what they did. The word *staff* was all-encompassing to Pastor Butcher and, consequently, to all of us.

Whenever good things would be reported, his strong advice was, "Never completely accept compliments for successes yourself. Find a way to pass the accolades around." *Together* was forever a synonym for *staff*. The friendships born there will last into eternity.

We shared a lot of laughter, both in the offices and on the platform. But Pastor Butcher had one rule: Never wit (a laugh at someone's expense no matter what the cost of dignity or position), only humor (warm and friendly, endorsing each other). No "put-downs" allowed.

In honor of the *staff* approach, I wrote a ditty one time, extolling the affection:

It's nice to have an unseen Friend
On whom you always can depend.
But sometimes, though, I must confess,
I'd like to have, in times of stress,
A face to see and a hand to grip.
That's what God calls "fellowship."

When the water rises around your
ship in the harbor, it rises around
every ship in the harbor.

Ministry is an attitude of mind and heart that relates
persons and things with action." At least that's how I
would "Reader's Digest" the Pastor Butcher concept of
service and ministry.

Ministry can well be defined in motive—it reaches out; it
doesn't pull in. Jesus seldom asked people for a commitment
without having given something of himself first. In fact,
Jesus most often asked people, "What can I do for you?" He
knelt and blessed their children, visited at their weddings,
listened to their problems, and affirmed their value and

self-worth. No wonder he had the whole town coming to his doorstep.

Pastor Butcher had some assignments for his staff that did not always resonate with great enthusiasm. For instance, he was adamant about all of us attending the annual Wesleyan pastors' conferences. I was just as resolute about not attending. "There are never any meetings addressing areas in my focus of ministry," I insisted. "I just don't get anything out of it. In my list of enjoyable things to do, it falls somewhere between dropping a bowling ball on my toe and eating Brussels sprouts."

He said firmly, "It's not about what you can get there; it's about what you can give. We have a big staff; none of them do. We get to fellowship together every day; they have no one close. Just go, and be a blessing." I did . . . and hope I was.

Another denomination was planting a new church about a mile from our property. I viewed that as competition, but Pastor Butcher saw it as an opportunity to assist in ministry. "This area is too big for us to handle all alone. We need help. God has sent these believers to assist us in this part of San Diego County."

When that same church had a work day, Pastor Butcher saw to it that not only did a group of Skyline men go to build, but our Skyline ladies prepared "lunch for the bunch." All of them.

That little church grew and prospered and eventually added an assisted living facility. It is no coincidence that Pastor and Mrs. Butcher later resided there in the Mount Miguel Covenant Village.

What goes around comes around.

Spiritual integrity is not an inheritance—each person must build it for himself.

Keep your soul moist."

That statement always got my attention. The visual picture of this concept is mesmerizing. By saying (and demonstrating), "Keep your soul moist," Pastor Butcher meant more than spritzing a little dewdrop here and a little dabber over there. He really intended for us to "Take a dip, immerse ourselves, and stand under the waterfall of grace for a while." There is no secondhand spiritual attainment available to any of us. God still works on a one-on-one basis.

He wants to do great things for us . . . and in us . . . and to us . . . and through us. We just have to get to the place where He can accomplish that. There was a grand old camp meeting song that was one of my favorites: "Standing under the Spout Where the Glory Comes Out." Pastor Butcher's admonition was simply "Get there."

Sometimes that moisture can come in difficult and abrasive situations. It's very important to let God do in your heart the things that ultimately are for your good, even if they humble you—or perhaps, *especially* if they humble you.

Here's another way to look at it. Pastor Butcher had a great analogy of the out-of-tune piano. He'd sit and play for a moment—beautiful chords and thrilling arpeggios. Then suddenly—a harsh, blatant chord that jarred the ear and disturbed the soul.

"Oops," he'd say, acting surprised. "This lovely instrument just went out of tune." A few more attempts at full chords and finger runs produced no different results. High notes and low notes—their combinations all were grating.

"Suppose we fix this piano up. Maybe the wood is too worn. Let's strip it and sand it and stain it and wax it and polish it." He hit the chords again—no change.

"Let's put a candelabra on it. That would beautify the appearance. Or perhaps hanging a chandelier over it . . . or what if we added a gorgeous bouquet of flowers?" He hit the chords again—still no change.

"The only hope is to call a master piano tuner. The problem is internal, not external. All the beautifying and behavior modification hasn't done a thing. The tuner can correct the trouble easily.

"But face this truth: The piano can go out of tune again. So what's the answer? Live with the Master Tuner near you at all times. That's the only way to 'keep your soul moist.'"

Humility is like underwear.
It should always be worn,
but never show.

Pastor Butcher started life by growing up in a wonderful Wesleyan Methodist parsonage. From his mother and father, Coral and Charles, he learned the secret of the "holy life." Then he spent five years at First Covenant Church in Minneapolis serving as youth pastor for Dr. Paul Rees. There he learned how to be a "man of the cloth."

That's also where he met Billy Graham, became part of the "team," and began the life of a traveling evangelist. He was with the Billy Graham team at the founding of Youth for Christ and in their early crusades. But, eventually, feeling that

God had called him to the pastorate, he left them and Skyline was born.

Nevertheless, through the years, those men stayed close friends with Pastor Butcher. Any time they were near San Diego, they'd call and Pastor Butcher would join them for breakfast and a morning of sharing stories from the "battle-front." Imagine my thrill as a young youth pastor to join in as a "fly on the wall."

When the Graham team planned a crusade in San Diego, they asked Pastor Butcher to head it up. He deferred. "No, you need a Baptist for that position. I know just the man. Let me be the crusade secretary. I can run the whole project for you from that position."

David (name changed to protect the guilty) was perfect—well dressed, man about town, hail fellow well met, and super-confident. He loved to brag about "knowing Billy." "I've even golfed with him and I can tell you what color shorts he wears—and they're boxers, by the way!"

Through all the campaign preparations, Pastor Butcher never mentioned to anyone his personal association and affiliation with Billy Graham. When Pastor Butcher walked into the big dinner gathering of seven hundred and fifty pastors, Cliff Barrows jumped up, shouting, "Orv! Over here!" George Beverly Shea likewise gave a basso greeting, and Billy Graham stood and hugged him. You can imagine the shock to David, who thought he was the only person in San Diego County to know "Billy."

At the Sunday afternoon rally at Jack Murphy Stadium, in front of fifty thousand people, Cliff talked about Pastor Butcher singing at his wedding, Bev mentioned that he and Pastor Butcher used to play together in front of a camp meeting tabernacle while their fathers preached inside. And Billy Graham publicly called him "one of the most focused and dedicated pastors I have ever known."

I once asked Pastor Butcher why he always called him "Dr. Graham" and never "Billy." I said, "If anyone has the right to his first name, it's you."

He smiled and said, "No . . . I know him too well to call him 'Billy.'"